P9-BXZ-688

FACILITATION SKILLS FOR TEAM LEADERS

Donald Hackett, Ph.D.
and Charles L. Martin, Ph.D.

A FIFTY-MINUTE™ SERIES BOOK

CRISP PUBLICATIONS, INC.
Menlo Park, California

FACILITATION SKILLS FOR TEAM LEADERS

Donald Hackett, Ph.D.
and Charles L. Martin, Ph.D.

CREDITS:
Editor: **Brenda Machosky**
Typesetting: **ExecuStaff**
Cover Design: **Carol Harris**
Artwork: **Ralph Mapson**

Copyright © 1993 Crisp Publications, Inc.
Printed in the United States of America by Bawden Printing Company.

English language Crisp books are distributed worldwide. Our major international distributors include:

CANADA: Reid Publishing Ltd., Box 69559—109 Thomas St., Oakville, Ontario, Canada L6J 7R4. TEL: (905) 842-4428, FAX: (905) 842-9327

Raincoast Books Distribution Ltd., 112 East 3rd Avenue, Vancouver, British Columbia, Canada V5T 1C8. TEL: (604) 873-6581, FAX: (604) 874-2711

AUSTRALIA: Career Builders, P.O. Box 1051, Springwood, Brisbane, Queensland, Australia 4127. TEL: 841-1061, FAX: 841-1580

NEW ZEALAND: Career Builders, P.O. Box 571, Manurewa, Auckland, New Zealand. TEL: 266-5276, FAX: 266-4152

JAPAN: Phoenix Associates Co., Mizuho Bldg. 2-12-2, Kami Osaki, Shinagawa-Ku, Tokyo 141, Japan. TEL: 3-443-7231, FAX: 3-443-7640

Selected Crisp titles are also available in other languages. Contact International Rights Manager Suzanne Kelly at (415) 323-6100 for more information.

Library of Congress Catalog Card Number 92-082933
Hackett, Donald and Charles L. Martin
Facilitation Skills for Team Leaders
ISBN 1-56052-199-6

This book is printed on recyclable paper with soy ink.

ABOUT THE BOOK

Facilitation Skills for Team Leaders is not like most books. It has a unique self-paced format that encourages a reader to become personally involved. Designed to be ''read with a pencil,'' there are an abundance of exercises, activities and assessments that invite participation.

The objective of this book is to provide a resource that will help people who are placed in the roles of facilitators build their skills to become more effective team leaders.

Facilitation Skills for Team Leaders can be used effectively in a number of ways. Here are some possibilities:

Individual Study. Because the book is self-instructional, all that is needed is a quiet place, some time and a pencil. Completing the activities and exercises should provide not only valuable feedback, but also practical ideas for identifying and developing facilitation skills.

Workshops and Seminars. The book is ideal for preassigned reading prior to a workshop or seminar. With the basics in hand, the quality of participation should improve. More time can be spent on concept extensions and applications during the program. The book is also effective when distributed at the beginning of a session.

Remote Location Training. Copies can be sent to those not able to attend ''home office'' training sessions.

Informal Study Groups. Thanks to the format, brevity and low cost, this book is ideal for ''brown-bag'' or other informal group sessions.

There are other possibilities that depend on the objectives of the user. One thing is certain: even after it has been read, this book will serve as excellent reference material that can be easily reviewed. Good luck!

ABOUT THE AUTHORS

Don Hackett

Don Hackett's rich management background in business and military organizations, combined with consulting and academic experience, provides a unique resource for his readers and audiences.

After receiving his Ph.D. in marketing and management in 1973 from the University of Oklahoma, Dr. Hackett joined the faculty of the College of Business Administration at the Wichita State University in Kansas. He was Director of Graduate Studies in Business for six years and is currently the Director of the Center for Management Development in the W. Frank Barton School of Business at WSU. He also consults and teaches in the area of quality improvement.

Dr. Hackett has written extensively in marketing and management, and authored *Franchising, Status, and Strategies*, published by the American Marketing Association.

Charles L. Martin

After earning a Ph.D. in marketing from Texas A&M University (1986), Charles L. Martin joined the faculty at Wichita State University, where he is currently an Associate Professor. At WSU, Dr. Martin's primary teaching duties involve courses in marketing management and services marketing. Dr. Martin has pioneered two courses at WSU focusing upon the marketing challenges faced by service organizations. His interest in service organizations has also translated into an ongoing research program examining the processes service businesses utilize to cement relationships with their customers. To date, Dr. Martin has published 9 books and more than 100 articles for both trade and academic audiences. In addition, he is currently serving as editor of *The Journal of Services Marketing*.

INTRODUCTION

This book is a practical, hands-on guide about teamwork in business—not how to form teams or how to delegate to teams, but how to *facilitate* organized teams as they solve complex and challenging problems and as they develop innovative ways to enhance productivity.

As sports coaches and knowledgeable sports enthusiasts are well aware, a successful team is one that accomplishes more than the sum of the team members' individual contributions. Championship teams focus on team objectives of winning; individual performances are only secondary considerations. Like sports organizations, increasingly businesses too are realizing the benefits of a team-oriented approach to accomplishing more. However, many businesses find the transition difficult—even painful—as performance evaluation systems, incentives, rewards, job descriptions and managerial styles are often still rooted in a perspective that recognizes the individual, but not the team. Consequently, it is possible to assemble a group of *individuals* with no guarantee that they will ever work together effectively as a team.

For supervisors, managers and executives sincerely committed to the process of transforming groups of employees into unified work teams, this book offers help. Useful concepts and tools are discussed throughout the book, with several quizzes and exercises interwoven to check for understanding and to develop valuable skills.

Thoughtful consideration of the ideas, concepts, and tools addressed in this book, coupled with a dedicated effort to answer the quiz questions and complete the exercises, should prepare any reader to be a more effective facilitator—which, in turn, will help to make teamwork a reality in any organization.

Donald Hackett & Charles L. Martin

CONTENTS

P A R T

I

Understanding Facilitation

BACKGROUND: THE TRANSFORMATION OF U.S. INDUSTRY

A transformation has been under way in American organizations since the early 1980s. This movement originates with an obsession for satisfying customer needs through quality products and services. Total Quality Management (TQM) is a common name for this approach, although other common acronyms are Total Quality Control (TQC), Continuous Quality Improvement (CQI), and Quality and Productivity Development (QPD).

This movement toward Total Quality Management has its roots in the continued trend toward globalization. As U.S. firms met growing international competition, they rediscovered that "quality" was the essential criteria of business success. Unfortunately, while relying upon hierarchical organizations led by command and control or authoritarian leaders, U.S. organizations found it increasingly difficult to compete. The transformation has manifested itself in leadership vision and culture, organizational restructuring, leadership style refinement, increased measurement of results, empowerment of workers, and an obsession with satisfying customers.

The vision, or dream, of what an organization could become plays a major role in the transformation. A "vision" is the ability to perceive something not actually visible. The leader of a group must develop and communicate the vision to organizational members. Such a vision typically includes an organizational mission, the customers' place, and the role of technology and innovation. This vision then encourages a culture that influences the way an organization acts.

The way an organization acts also depends upon its structure and its culture. Organizational structure refers to the formally defined relationships of jobs within the company, i.e., who is supervised by whom, who is responsible for work tasks, and so on. Organizational "culture" consists of the attitudes, values, beliefs and behaviors of a group of people. Increasingly, the winning culture is one that places high value on customers, employees involvement, innovation, creativity, risk taking and quality in both products and services.

BACKGROUND: THE TRANSFORMATION OF U.S. INDUSTRY (continued)

To become more competitive, U.S. organizations began to "level" or flatten organization structures. This flattening was made possible as automation decreased the need for middle managers. Concomitant with organizational changes came leadership refinements. Leaders have changed from an authoritarian leadership style to a participatory or coaching style that draws upon the insight, experience, motivation and intelligence of their workers. Leaders have found that authoritarian leadership styles are less effective in motivating workers and implementing change. Workers have increasingly resisted being a "pair of hands" and yearn for greater involvement in their organizations. Worker empowerment means less resistance to change since people tend to support what they create. Thus, an increasingly common tool for creating an involvement culture is the use of worker teams.

The positive role of worker groups involved in enhancing morale and productivity has been known for years. However, only in the last decade has the team concept been integrated into organizational structures. Since worker involvement is a cornerstone in quality improvement, the growth of work teams closely correlates with the growth of the quality improvement transformation.

The ability to measure "value added" improvements and to retain gains is another manifestation of TQM. The adage "you can't manage what you can't measure" has become part of the TQM culture. Thus, in order to improve, quality organizations rely heavily on traditional, yet simple, tools and statistical measures.

The final component of transformed organizations is a near fanatical commitment to satisfy their customers' needs. The organization adopts a customer-driven philosophy that acts as the catalyst for innovation and improvements in quality throughout the organization.

Quality Improvement Process

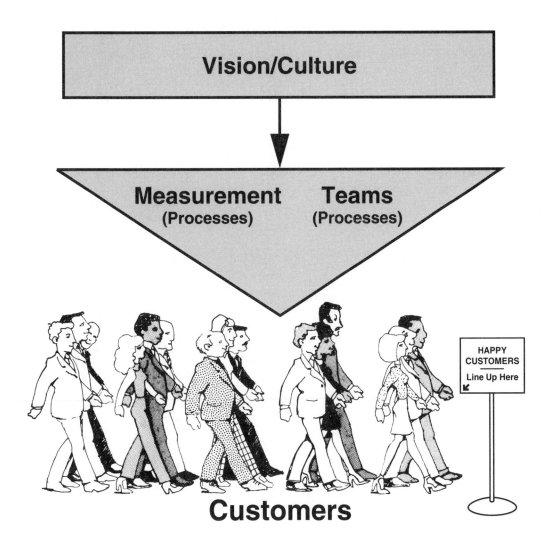

WHY FACILITATION?

When organizations move toward employee involvement, either formally or informally, group dynamics become a major factor in improvement. In facilitation exercises, the facilitator is responsible for providing a structure so that the team can be successful. Note that in traditional hierarchical organizations, individual rather than group work is the rule. Even when groups come together in traditional organizations, the environment tends to be one-way communication in a presentation format. Thus, most leaders do not fully understand group dynamics and therefore lack the skills needed to transform groups of individuals into effective teams. This brings us to:

Two Key Definitions

> *Team:* A collection of people (usually 5–9) who rely on cooperation, trust and communication in order to achieve their goals and objectives.
>
> *Facilitator:* An individual who is responsible for structuring teams, groups or task forces, and their activities so as to allow for their success in attaining organizational goals and objectives.

Teams can be permanent or ad hoc; they can be formally integrated into the organizational chart or an addendum; they can be fully empowered to make decisions or serve in an advisory capacity. Common names for teams today are Quality Improvement Teams (QIT), quality circles, cross-functional teams, task forces, lead teams, task teams, work teams, process improvement teams and project teams.

TWO STYLES OF LEADERSHIP

LEADERSHIP AND FACILITATION

When one speaks of facilitation, the word can be applied at different levels. For example, in terms of leadership style, a major trend is to reposition leaders from an authoritarian to a facilitative (coaching) style. A comparison of authoritarian and facilitative leadership styles is illustrated below.

Authoritarian Style	Facilitative/Coaching
► Task oriented	► Quality oriented
► One-way communicators	► Encourages empowerment of workers to solve problems and make decisions
► Subordinates are a "pair of hands"	
► Uses direct and implied threats	► Emphasizes trust, innovation, and risk taking
► Makes all decisions	► Defines jobs broadly and utilizes cross training
► Uses policy and structure	► Works for consensus from teams
► Uses extrinsic rewards to motivate (e.g., money, promotions, etc.)	► Skilled at getting teams involved in improvement actions
► Good at "office politics"	► Uses intrinsic motivation (e.g., praise, achievement, etc.)
► Considered the "expert"	
► Pushes change directed from top	► Works to initiate change through groups
► Works "one on one" with subordinates	► Works across team boundaries to get team resources
► Subordinates are to please boss	► Employees serve group's needs

WHAT FACILITATORS DO

The involvement of teams empowered to enhance quality has spawned a relatively new set of skills among leaders. These skills are characterized as facilitation skills. Facilitation can take on different forms in an organization. For example, executives often use ''facilitators'' to bring focus in their strategic planning sessions. Additionally, market researchers use focus groups to determine customer needs. These sessions are headed by facilitators. Arbitrators in labor issues often facilitate the issues discussed between parties representing labor and management. The U.S. Army uses a facilitator style to evaluate soldier training in After Action Reviews (AARs).

Effective leaders are increasingly those people who are capable of facilitating change and improvement through team empowerment. ''Empowerment'' is to enable the team to perform through the sharing of decision-making authority. The quality improvement philosophy places emphasis on continuous improvement through involvement of work teams. Teams need facilitators to be successful.

Facilitators are primarily organizers and communicators, with a special expertise in group dynamics. They ensure there is a culture of two-way expressive involvement that emphasizes active listening as well as trusting communication among the participants. They are encouragers of team behaviors in planning, organizing, disciplining and monitoring the team's activities. They must have patience, a tolerance for ambiguity, and the need to develop a sense of timing that aids in knowing when to push for more ideas, more information, and more participation, and—equally important—when *not* to push. Finally, they should have the ability to organize, handle details and bring events to closure.

Formal Facilitators

Another definition of facilitator is the position title within a group or team. The facilitator in a work team is the person responsible for focusing the group's efforts toward its objectives. For example, in a Quality Improvement Team (QIT), there are designated roles. Typically, you will minimally find a team leader, facilitator and (five to nine) team members. The supervisor may or may not be a part of the team. If the supervisor is a part of the team, he may act as the facilitator, the team leader or perform as a team member. The facilitator may also be the team leader, or designated as a ''stand-alone'' position. In some larger organizations, full-time facilitators are used to assist work teams. (In these cases, facilitators may assist six to eight teams on a full-time basis.)

Regardless, the facilitator's role is to provide the structure and focus for the team. This book concentrates on this role and specific facilitator skills and behaviors in moving the team through its decision-making steps.

DESIRABLE FACILITATING BEHAVIORS CHECKLIST

Below is a more specific list of desirable facilitative behaviors. Place a check next to each behavior at which now you excel. After reading this book and practicing the exercises you should be able to confidently place checks next to each of these skills.

- ☐ Planning for a team meeting
- ☐ Knowing how to ask questions
- ☐ Being an active listener
- ☐ Knowing how to use a flip chart
- ☐ Remaining neutral on content issues
- ☐ Encouraging open communication
- ☐ Encouraging team problem-solving
- ☐ Knowing how to lead using group problem-solving tools
- ☐ Encouraging team decision making
- ☐ Sensitive to capturing and maintaining documentation
- ☐ Clarifying, sharing, and disseminating information
- ☐ Maintaining team focus
- ☐ Giving verbal and written feedback
- ☐ Communicating thoughts and feelings clearly
- ☐ Developing a culture of teamwork
- ☐ Obtaining team resources
- ☐ Obtaining technical expertise for team
- ☐ Striving for consensus decision making
- ☐ Tolerating and smoothing conflict
- ☐ Linking teams to management

PUTTING YOUR FACILITATION SKILLS IN ACTION

Do you have what it takes to be a top-flight facilitator? Here are a few comments that inexperienced, ineffective facilitators might make. In the blank spaces that follow each comment, write what you think an experienced, effective facilitator might say instead.

1. "What should we talk about in our meeting today?"

_____

2. "Here's how I think we should solve this problem . . ."

_____

3. "Rita, that idea makes no sense at all. You'll have to do better than that."

_____

4. "Great idea, Fred. That is obviously the best solution offered today!"

_____

5. "Okay, it's time to vote. Who is in favor of Rita's proposed solution? Who prefers Fred's?"

_____

6. "We tried that approach two years ago and it did not work."

_____

7. "We have listed eight possible solutions. Which is the _worst_ idea we can safely eliminate from further consideration?"

_____

8. "No Bob, we can't discuss that. It's not relevant to the issue at hand."

_____

AUTHORS' RECOMMENDED ALTERNATIVES

Of course there are several ways experienced facilitators might rephrase the previous comments, but here are some recommended alternatives.

1. Instead of: "What should we talk about in our meeting today?" consider . . .

   "Did everyone get a copy of today's meeting agenda that I distributed last week?"

2. Instead of: "Here's how I think we should solve this problem . . ." consider . . .

   "Now that we have reached an agreement as to what the problem is, what are some possible solutions?"

3. Instead of: "Rita, that idea makes no sense at all. You'll have to do better than that." consider . . .

   "I'm sorry Rita, but I don't understand your point. Could you explain it again, please?"

4. Instead of: "Great idea, Fred. That is obviously the best solution offered today!" consider . . .

   "Thanks for your input, Fred. Would anyone care to comment on Fred's proposal?"

5. Instead of: "Okay, it's time to vote. Who is in favor of Rita's proposed solution? Who prefers Fred's?" consider . . .

   "We have discussed the merits of both Rita's and Fred's proposals. Is there any way we might be able to combine the advantages of both ideas?"

6. Instead of: "We tried that approach two years ago and it did not work." consider . . .

   "Allow me to write that approach on the flip chart. Are there any other possibilities we might add to the list?"

7. Instead of: "We have listed eight possible solutions. Which is the *worst* idea we can safely eliminate from further consideration?" consider . . .

   "We have listed eight possible solutions. Unless someone has a ninth option, please list on separate sheets of paper the four solutions you think would be the most viable. We will then discuss the top choices in greater detail."

8. Instead of: "No Bob, we can't discuss that. It's not relevant to the issue at hand." consider . . .

   "I see your point Bob, but could you hold that thought until next week when we are scheduled to address that issue?"

HOW FACILITATION DIFFERS FROM TRAINING AND PRESENTING

Training, public presentations and facilitating share some common behavior and skills and often complement each other; but these are distinctly different developmental activities. Illustrated below are some traits of each.

Training	Presenting	Facilitation
Participants are present to learn.	Audience is present to receive prepared remarks.	Participants are members of teams whose mission is to recommend quality improvement.
Objectives are based upon learning.	Objectives are based on what is to be communicated—i.e., sell, inform, motivate, describe.	Objectives are based on process improvements.
Lesson plans are prepared to enhance learning structure.		
Instructor is a catalyst for learning.	Presenter's outline is to structure logical presentation.	An agenda is used to structure the meeting for effectiveness.
Instructor asks questions to evaluate learning.	Presenter primarily answers rather than asks questions.	Questions are used to develop individual involvement.
Visual and training aids (tapes, films, cases, roleplays) are used to illustrate learning points.	Visual aids are used to present data, (charts, graphs, tables).	Flip chart is used to record team member inputs and ideas.
Involvement (experiential learning) is used to learn from others' experience and retain interest.	Data, charts, graphs are used to support message or recommendations.	Facilitator teaches members to use tools for team problem solving.
Number of participants varies; usually under 50.	Communication is largely one way from presenter to audience.	Facilitator manages the meeting structure, not content. Team size is typically 5–9 members.
	Group can be any size.	May present the team's improvement recommendations to management.

QUIZ: TRAINING, PRESENTING OR FACILITATING

Check your understanding of the appropriateness of each of the three developmental methods by placing a ''T'' next to the scenario below in which *training* would be most appropriate, a ''P'' next to those that lend themselves to *presenting* and an ''F'' next to those calling for *facilitation*.

_____ **1.** A new cashier needs to learn how to operate the cash register.

_____ **2.** The members of the sales force doesn't know the technical specifications of a new product they are to sell.

_____ **3.** The company must decide how best to respond to customers' requests for quicker delivery.

_____ **4.** Retail clerks must be made aware of weekly sale items.

_____ **5.** A recently hired quality-control inspector doesn't understand how to fill out the detailed quality report.

_____ **6.** Management is concerned that too many raw materials are being wasted during the final week of each quarter, but doesn't know why the increased waste occurs or what to do about it.

_____ **7.** Employees are confused about the changes in the company's health-care insurance coverage.

_____ **8.** Production foremen have noticed an uneven flow of materials and work-in-process throughout the plant. They are concerned that this may create production inefficiencies.

_____ **9.** A foreman notices a worker using a drill press that is not properly adjusted.

_____ **10.** A competitor introduces a new product with distinguishable features that consumers seem to appreciate. However, the feasibility of producing a similar product with comparable features is uncertain.

Congratulations if your answers match these!

1. T, 2. P, 3. F, 4. P, 5. T, 6. F, 7. P, 8. F, 9. T, 10. F.

THE FACILITATOR: MANAGING STRUCTURE, NOT CONTENT

Because the facilitator is visibly positioned in the group, this person has the ability to bias the team either intentionally or unintentionally. Thus, the role of facilitator is to manage the meeting *structure* while remaining neutral regarding the meeting *content*. The meeting content is the responsibility of the team. This position of neutrality must be understood and practiced by the facilitator if the team's potential is to be fully reached. The facilitator who personally moves into heavy involvement of the team's content issues runs the risk of reducing team involvement, trust and openness. Below are definitions of these two concepts.

Structure Versus Content

Structure: Fulfills the "how" questions. How the meeting's issues and subjects are dealt with; how the meeting proceeds in terms of agenda and team tools; how discussions take place; how decision tools are used; how formats, flip charts, and involvement take place; how the meeting's physical environment will be arranged.

Content: Answers the "what" questions. What are the meeting's subject, issues, problems, analysis, recommendations, and supporting data. What issues will be dealt with in what sequence.

As shown by the following illustration, the team's effectiveness is heightened when team members understand both structure and content issues.

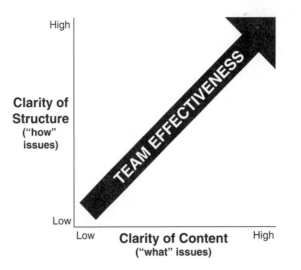

QUIZ: CONTENT OR STRUCTURE?

Check your understanding of structure and content with this quiz. Determine whether the activity is part of content or structure. Place a check mark under the appropriate column.

	Content	Structure
1. Development and distribution of team meeting agenda and preparation of room	_____	_____
2. Statements of meeting objectives	_____	_____
3. Discussion involving clarification of team objective	_____	_____
4. Cost information on purchase of air filters	_____	_____
5. Progress report on the factory's air quality	_____	_____
6. Moving into subgroups to discuss possible improvement solutions	_____	_____
7. A brainstorming session to develop improvement ideas	_____	_____
8. A free-flowing discussion resulting from facilitator questions	_____	_____
9. Use of a flowchart to describe a job process developed by the team	_____	_____
10. A presentation of existing company safety policies by a team member	_____	_____
11. Designated individual recording group's discussion points on a flip chart	_____	_____
12. Report detailing company's expected safety budget	_____	_____
13. Summarizing and clarifying team decision	_____	_____
14. A team recommendation made to management	_____	_____

Answers: Issues 2, 3, 4, 5, 10, 12, and 14 are content issues. The others pertain to structure.

PART

II

Team Involvement, Decision Making, and Dynamics

ENCOURAGING PARTICIPATION

Eight people in a team are smarter than any one person. However, to reach the best decision, the team members must be in an environment that encourages them to express their thoughts, ideas and experiences.

Experienced facilitators will tell you that the greatest and most important tool in successful facilitation is gaining involvement and participation from the group members. The measure of the team's success largely derives from both the quantity and quality of the team's involvement. In every stage of team development, involvement is the essential element. The team's level of involvement will depend on several factors including the creation of a climate of trust and openness to help the team work more effectively as it matures.

Perhaps the two most important skills of the facilitator are her or his ability to:

1. **ASK QUESTIONS**

2. **RECORD THE MEMBERS' RESPONSES**

SKILL #1: HOW TO ASK QUESTIONS

Do you remember when you were a student and the teacher would unexpectedly call out your name for the answer to a question? If you didn't know the answer you probably experienced an emotional roller coaster ranging from surprise to panic, and finally to embarrassment or even humiliation. As a result, you may have become less interested in the topic and intimidated by the discussion. Certainly, you were less likely to become a relaxed participant in the discussion. Accomplished facilitators never create unpleasant feelings in attaining involvement. Instead, they attempt to create fulfillment and satisfaction within the team as a result of participation.

RULES FOR ASKING NONTHREATENING QUESTIONS

Following are general rules for effectively asking nonthreatening questions to get participation.

Rule 1

Initially ask each question of the entire team.

Example: What are the possible reasons for increased scrap levels during the last ten days of the quarter? (Do *not* say, "Jane, what are the possible reasons for increased scrap levels in the last ten days of the quarter?")

Rule 2

Pause and allow the team members time to consider the question.

Note: Some facilitators become anxious if a question does not elicit an immediate response. If this happens to you, relax; your team members are thinking.

Rule 3

If a team member responds, acknowledge the remark and explore the response further if possible or necessary. For example:

Team member: "One of the reasons we have more scrap relates to working overtime to meet production quotas."
Facilitator: "Overtime huh? Why would overtime create more scrap?"
Team member: "Well, overtime work causes fatigue and carelessness, resulting in more scrap."

Rule 4

If no one responds in a reasonable amount of time, look for nonverbal signals from a team member who is wanting to be involved—i.e., eye contact, a forward lean, an uplifted eyebrow. Then, go to that person by name.

Example: "Carol, you look as if you have something to offer here. Can you help us out? In your opinion, why does our scrap count go up during the last days of each quarter?"

Rule 5 If no one responds to a question, consider rewording the question or asking if the question needs clarification.

Example: "Have I explained this clearly?" (rather than, "Do you understand?")

Rule 6 Avoid biased questions.

Example: "What may be causing the problem?" (instead of, "Is the problem caused by untrained workers or by inferior materials?" The problem may be caused by one or more other factors!)

Rule 7 Avoid too many "yes/no" questions, which limit discussion.

Example: "Is the increased scrap level due to worker fatique?" (You will probably get a "yes" or "no" answer, but little discussion.)

Rule 8 Avoid questions that may put team members on the defensive.

Example: "Why are scrap levels in the factory increasing?" (rather than, "Bob, why does your department's scrap level seem to continuously increase?")

Rule 9 Refrain from the temptation of initially asking "by name" questions to get people's attention or to punish their inattention. Such actions by the facilitator cause resentment and further noninvolvement by team members.

Hint: Be careful of praising questions or responses of participants with words such as "That's a good question" or "what a great idea." Other members not receiving such praise may interpret their question or response as being less valuable.

TYPES OF QUESTIONS TO ASK

There are five categories of questions that skilled facilitators use to gain greater participation by their team members. These types of questions include:

1. Open Ended
2. Greater Response
3. Redirection
4. Feedback and Clarification
5. Close-Ended

Facilitators typically need to use the first four question types frequently and the close-ended probe only under special circumstances. Each of these five types of questions are discussed below.

1. Open-Ended Questions

An open-ended question is one that cannot be answered with a single word or phrase such as "yes" or "no." Open-ended questions are quite powerful because they stimulate thinking, encourage greater discussion, and discourage team members from prematurely taking definitive positions on issues not yet thoroughly discussed. They typically begin with words such as "how," "what" and "why." Here are a few examples of open-ended questions.

- *How* do the rest of you feel about this?

- *How* will this solution impact you?

- *How* do you want to evaluate this idea?

- *What* are your observations of these three potential causes?

- *What* can be done to eliminate this type of mistake?

- *What* happens if we don't solve the problem?

- *Why* are waste and spoilage up even after our new equipment purchase?

- *Why* are we having problems with our billing system?

- *Why* did you say "step 3" is so crucial to the process?

2. Greater Response Questions

An adaptation of the open-ended probe is the *Greater Response Question.* In order to gain understanding and add depth to the team's involvement, facilitators need to know how to use three words to draw out greater information. These words are ''describe,'' ''tell'' and ''explain.'' For example:

- ''Can you *describe* how we typically handle telephone complaints?''

- ''Could you *tell* us more about our customers' reaction to the policy?''

- ''Would you please *explain* to us why our new system still costs more to operate?''

3. Redirection Questions

A team member will often ask questions of the facilitator as a follow-up of a remark made by him or another team member. It is important to recall that the facilitator should be neutral in content and proactive in structure. If the question relates to structure, answer it. However, if the question relates to content, consider redirecting it to other team members. For example, a team member might ask you, ''Why do you think our costs increased after the new equipment was installed?'' As the facilitator, you might respond by appropriately redirecting the question in the following ways:

- ''What do the rest of you think about that?''

- ''That relates to what Helen suggested earlier. Helen, what are your thoughts?''

- ''That question needs to be answered by someone experienced in that area. Is there anyone who has worked with the new equipment?''

TYPES OF QUESTIONS TO ASK (continued)

4. Feedback and Clarification Questions

At certain times in meetings, the facilitator needs to bring closure or clarification to a topic being discussed. At the same time it is important that all team members are together in understanding the issue's status. At such times, clarification and feedback questions are appropriate. For example:

- "Let's see Liz, if I heard you right; you are saying . . .?"

- "Where are we; will someone summarize our position?"

- "Who can paraphrase our position regarding recent productivity losses in the foundry?"

- "You indicated a desire to analyze possible solutions to our automation errors; what area did we agree to brainstorm first?"

5. Close-Ended Questions

The close-ended question is often asked too frequently by inexperienced facilitators. These questions typically result in a "yes," "no" or short response from participants and provide little involvement. Use these questions infrequently and for clarification since they typically add little to the discussion process. Here are some examples:

- "Has this issue been explained clearly?"

- "What was the error rate?"

- "Who is the fluid controller on the first shift?"

- "How many reworks did we have?"

PUTTING QUESTIONS TOGETHER

Facilitators gain skill in involvement when they can piggyback several questions back to back for enhanced involvement. The following dialogue between a facilitator and two team members illustrates a sequence of four questions and responses using the "chain-of-questions" technique.

Chain-of-Questions Technique

Facilitator: Can anyone explain why our scrap levels tend to increase during the last ten days of the quarter?

Carol: One of the reasons we have more scrap relates to working overtime to meet production quotas; working overtime means fatigued workers and sloppier work.

Facilitator: In your estimation, is overtime work the total explanation for increased scrap?

Carol: No, typically overtime accounts for only 1 to 2 percent more scrap than during regular hours.

Facilitator: What are other explanations for the increased scrap levels in the latter part of the quarter?

Michael: I know of another possible explanation. Production holds all scrap numbers that are coded "machine malfunctioned" until the last week of the quarter. They then record these in the scrap account because it is more convenient.

Facilitator: Okay, can anyone tell us what percentage "machine malfunctioned" codes are of the total scrap account?

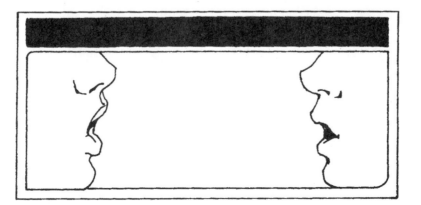

QUIZ: THE MATCH GAME!

Test your grasp of the various types of questions a skilled facilitator might use by matching the example questions in the left column below with the correct question types from the right column.

<table>
<tr><td colspan="2">Example Questions</td><td>Question Types</td></tr>
<tr><td>1. _____</td><td>Why do you believe delivery will take three weeks?</td><td>A. Redirection</td></tr>
<tr><td>2. _____</td><td>Three weeks, huh?</td><td>B. Open ended</td></tr>
<tr><td>3. _____</td><td>I can't answer that. Phil, perhaps you could help us?</td><td>C. Clarification or Feedback</td></tr>
<tr><td>4. _____</td><td>Okay, what are the potential problem areas we have identified so far today?</td><td>D. Greater response</td></tr>
<tr><td>5. _____</td><td>Thanks for your suggestion. Would that alternative offer additional benefits? And would these benefits be cost-efficient?</td><td>E. Chain-of-questions technique</td></tr>
</table>

Answers: If your answers are as follows, congratulations!
1. B. 2. D. 3. A. 4. C. 5. E.

BODY LANGUAGE AND FACILITATION

While most of us initially think of verbal skills as the major facilitation skill, you should also consider the role of nonverbal or body language messages. In a meeting, these nonverbal messages are constantly flowing from team members, the team leader and the facilitator.

The astute facilitator will refrain from sending signals that may be interpreted negatively by the receiver. Look at the example in Figure A. This figure shows a closed posture (notice the arms), which tends to indicate a closed mind, lack of confidence, or inattentiveness. This type of body language inhibits or discourages communication.

Figure B is a good example of positive body language. This facilitator uses arms and hands to indicate an open signal, which invites involvement and communication.

Figure A   **Figure B**

EXERICISE: INTERPRETING BODY LANGUAGE

Here are some other examples of desirable and undesirable nonverbal behaviors. In the space provided, note your impressions of how these behaviors might be interpreted by the team member speaking at the time.

1. Facilitator looks at her watch.

_____

2. Facilitator gazes out the window for several seconds.

_____

3. Facilitator yawns.

_____

4. Facilitator leans forward and maintains eye contact with speaking team member.

_____

5. Facilitator scratches his chin and nods.

_____

6. Facilitator makes _brief_ notes on his notepad.

_____

7. Facilitator makes _lengthy_ notes on her notepad.

_____

8. Facilitator laughs or smiles.

_____

9. Facilitator drums pencil on table.

_____

AUTHORS' SUGGESTED RESPONSES

Now compare your impressions with those of the authors . . .

1. Facilitator looks at her watch.

   "You wish I'd stop talking. You're thinking about what you'll do later today."

2. Facilitator gazes out the window for several seconds.

   "You're daydreaming and not listening to what I have to say. Why should I bother to participate?"

3. Facilitator yawns.

   "You're bored with what I'm saying."

4. Facilitator leans forward and maintains eye contact with speaking team member.

   "You must be interested in what I have to say."

5. Facilitator scratches his chin and nods.

   "I must have said something very insightful!"

6. Facilitator makes *brief* notes on his notepad.

   "You must want to remember what I'm saying."

7. Facilitator makes *lengthy* notes on her notepad.

   "How can you attentively listen to me and write at the same time?"

8. Facilitator laughs or smiles.

   "You're obviously listening to me, otherwise you would not have detected the humor in my comment."

   OR

   "Are you laughing at me? I am trying to be serious. What is so funny?"

9. Facilitator drums pencil on table.

   "You are impatient. You do not like my ideas. It is obvious that you want me to shut up."

SKILL #2: RECORD THE TEAM'S EFFORT

A staple tool in the facilitator's life is the flip chart (newsprint flip chart displayed on an easel). Flip charts are used to record ideas, possible solutions, comparisons and decisions. Thus they act as the team focus and memory. Flip charts encourage participation because of their flexibility and easy recordability. First, because they are portable, flip charts can be used virtually anywhere, from the factory floor to the mountain retreat. Second, the pages from flip charts serve as the team minutes and memory, thus reducing the irritation of developing minutes. Third, and most importantly, the flip chart encourages involvement! The essence of the team concept is empowerment and participation. When an individual participates and the remarks are captured, the flip chart record serves as a visual reminder of that involvement while creating a group focus. Other advantages of flip chart use are:

► Giving a sense of progress

► Enhancing creativity through piggybacking of ideas

► Keeping the team focused on discussion

► Allowing latecomers the opportunity to catch up

The Role of the Recorder

When using the flip chart for team actions, the facilitator may choose to designate a team member as recorder. This is often done when the facilitator is a poor speller or messy writer. Recorders are also used when there is a heavy volume of recorded discussion and the facilitator needs to focus solely on the team activities.

Before the beginning of the session, facilitators who designate a recorder must properly coach the recorder on neutrality. Given the recorder's visually predominant position, it is easy and sometimes tempting to move from a recorder's role to unduly influencing content. Recorders must assume the facilitator's position of neutrality regarding content. Additionally, overzealous recorders can upstage the facilitator's role if the facilitator does not adequately define the recorder's responsibilities. When using the flip chart, it is recommended that facilitators stand up next to the flip chart even when a recorder is used.

The recorder, using a flip chart, must be sensitive to the ego needs of the participants. When recording, attempt to use the exact words of the person speaking. A recorder who takes the liberty of rephrasing a team member's words runs the risks of implying the contributor is inarticulate or even worse, that his idea is not valuable. If some team members' remarks are lengthy, simply ask them if you might rephrase their remarks for recording purposes. They will always say ''yes.''

> **HINT:** Consider rotating recorders for further involvement of team members.

HOW TO USE THE FLIP CHART

Here are a few suggestions that will help to increase the effectiveness of the flip chart and make it easier to use.

Posture

- Stand facing the group and to the side of the flip chart when facilitating

- Write on the flip chart with your body at an angle to participants

- Do not turn your back to the group while recording

- Ensure that all participants can see the flip chart

Recording

- Use a heading on each sheet

- Print in block letters 1 1/2 to 2 inches high

- Print as legibly as possible but do not be overly concerned about neatness or spelling

- Limit recording from 5 to 9 lines per page

- Strive to use participants' exact words when recording

- Leave 2 to 3 inches between lines

- Use ''bullets'' to denote each input if only a few points will be made; otherwise number the inputs

- Consider leaving the bottom one-fifth of sheet blank

- Use black, dark blue, green or purple felt markers for recording; use red, orange and yellow for highlighting

- Highlight by use of underlining, circles, bullets and use of contrasting color

- Use abbreviations liberally, e.g., ↑ (increase), ↓ (decrease), > (greater than), < (less than)

- Use diagrams when appropriate

Common Questions Asked By A Recorder

- Does this capture what you said?

- Can I paraphrase that by saying . . .

- Would you summarize that in a phrase or two for the record?

- What do you mean by that?

Displaying and Storing Recorded Sheets

- Practice tearing off sheets

- Attach sheets to the wall in sequence with masking tape*

- Store sheets flat or roll up and secure with a rubber band

- Label rolled sheets on the outside with topic and meeting date

*WARNING: Always check to see if the facility will allow flip chart sheets to be taped to walls. With fabric-type walls, straight pins or thumb tacks work well. Never write on flip chart pages attached to the wall; the ink may bleed through and damage the surface.

MAKING DECISIONS

Teams may be established with different objectives. A team within the accounting department can be charged continuously to improve its automation processes. In such cases, it is dubbed a process-improvement team. As such, it is a semipermanent team that consistently addresses automation improvement within the department. Another team in the organization might have the responsibility to solve the impact of the Americans with Disabilities Act on facility accessibility to disabled workers. This team has a one-time duty and will then be disbanded. Consequently, the steps these two teams go through may differ slightly. The following illustration is a schematic of the traditional steps teams move through in making decisions regarding improvement.

The Six Steps of the Team Problem-Solving Process

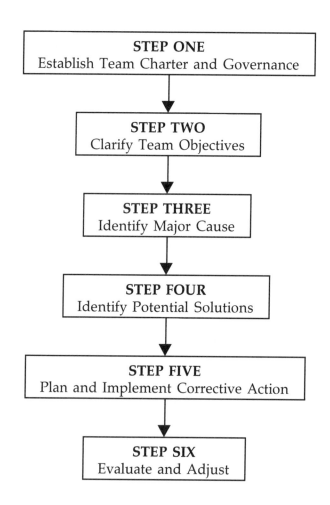

STEP ONE
Establish Team Charter and Governance

STEP TWO
Clarify Team Objectives

STEP THREE
Identify Major Cause

STEP FOUR
Identify Potential Solutions

STEP FIVE
Plan and Implement Corrective Action

STEP SIX
Evaluate and Adjust

The facilitator has several responsibilities regarding the team's movement through these steps. Again, note that the facilitator is not responsible for the content of the team's issues, but the structure. The facilitator should:

- Ensure the team understands the problem-solving steps

- Follow the steps in sequence

- Not allow individuals or the team to take shortcuts

- Ensure consensus after each step

- Train team members on use of team tools

- Help the group move through obstacles

- Document results of each step

- Keep the team focused on steps and overall objective

- Encourage the team toward closure

SIX-STEP PROBLEM-SOLVING PROCESS

Let's now take a closer look at what should occur in each step of the team's problem-solving process and what role the facilitator plays.

STEP ONE: Establish Team Charter and Governance

The team charter is the charge or mission given to the team. This charter typically originates from management or a management-designated sponsor such as the Quality Steering Committee (QSC). The charter typically includes the team's mission, background information, its authority, duties and reporting responsibilities. It may also include team member appointees, budget and a milestone chart or schedule. The facilitator should act as a catalyst to ensure the team both understands and agrees with its charter and mission. If not, the team or facilitator should seek clarification from the sponsor.

Team governance is an essential first step for team success. Without governance, the team's efforts are likely to be disorganized, or even chaotic. *Robert's Rules of Order* (available in most public libraries), is one example of a governance document. The insightful facilitator will ensure the team develops a viable set of team rules and procedures. The facilitator also will make sure that team members understand the rules and do not feel intimidated by them. Some of these governance issues that need addressing are:

✔ Who picks team members? How are members rotated or replaced?

✔ Are necessary skills and knowledge represented?

✔ How is time off from jobs handled?

✔ How is the team leader chosen? For how long?

✔ Who is responsible for meeting notices, agenda preparation, and team minutes?

✔ Who communicates with the sponsor? How often?

✔ What part of the team's work, if any, will be conducted individually or by subcommittees?

✔ How often will the team meet? How long?

✔ What represents a team quorum?

✔ How will team members' excessive absences be handled?

✔ Will individuals other than team members be notified of meetings?

✔ What represents consensus? How is it attained? Is voting allowed?

✔ Does anyone have veto power?

✔ What is the "team recommendations" report format?

A team charter addresses many of these governance issues with others addressed during initial group meetings. Here is an example of a charter for an organization's Safety and Health Quality Improvement Team.

Team Charter

Mission: Reduce the incidence of injuries resulting in workers' compensation claims.

Authority: The Quality Steering Committee (QSC) authorizes this team be formed and have access to meeting rooms, all workers' compensation company files, and staff needed to assist in interpretation of data and typing of recommendations.

Duties: Injuries are a personal and financial hardship to all parties involved. The team is asked to meet weekly to collect and analyze data and make recommendations to the QSC of potential solutions that will reduce these injuries. All data and documentation will be retained in team files and handled in a confidential manner.

Team Members:

Leader: Lois Childers
Facilitator: Margaret Graham
Members: Liz Brown, Dae Chung, Mary Gomez, Rex Graff, Bob Lutz

Resources: An initial budget of $1,500 is allocated. Additional resources can be requested through QSC.

Schedule: Quarterly reports are to be made to QSC. It is anticipated that initial recommendations will be made within 9 months.

SIX-STEP PROBLEM-SOLVING PROCESS (continued)

STEP TWO: Clarify Team Objectives

The team objectives are a further refinement of the team mission. For example, the team mission is to reduce workers' compensation claims in the plant. The team might further focus that mission into an objective of reducing workers' compensation claims by 30 percent. Thus the mission gives broad direction; the objective gives specific direction.

As a facilitator, you will find teams have a propensity to quickly move through step two. Be alert to this tendency and work to slow team efforts in this step. Proper attention to setting objectives tends to be hard work. It requires intense collaboration and reclarification. Experienced facilitators recommend that up to 30 percent of a team's total time be invested in step two. Why? If the team's objective is not clearly understood by all, it will most likely result in a "stuck" group in later steps.

The objective can be stated in one of three ways: the traditional statement, as a question, or in a situational statement. Examples of each of these three formats follow.

Traditional: To reduce workers' compensation claims by 30 percent during the next 18 months.

Question: How can we reduce workers' compensation claims by 30 percent during the next 18 months?

Situational: Our objective is to reduce workers' compensation claims by 30 percent during the next 18 months even though we will be adding another 150 untrained workers in our most demanding assembly area.

STEP THREE: Identify Major Causes

Step three represents the analysis segment of group problem solving. Team members are also prone to pay only cursory attention to this step in anticipation of moving to the solutions of step four. Again, slow the team down and focus adequate attention on the analysis required for effective problem solving.

Team problem-solving tools begin to play an increasingly important role in this step. For example, given a mission and objective, the team members will be confronted with several tasks. First, they will need to collect and analyze data. Then they will need to break the data down into ''bite size'' bits. Next they will need to establish data patterns and trends. Lastly, taking this data into consideration, they can brainstorm all potential causes and then establish and test for the root cause or causes.

The tools most frequently used in step three include histograms and graphs, brainstorming, cause-and-effect diagrams, flowcharting, and pareto analysis.

Continuing with our example of workers' compensation claims, step three might result in the following findings.

Workers' Compensation Findings

- 92% of all claims are from factory floor workers

- Factory floor workers' claims by category are:

Type of Injury	Number (or frequency)
Back related	56
Hand and arm	20
Hearing	10
Foot and leg	7
Vision	6
Stress related	4

- Workers' compensation back-related injuries findings:

  94% from lifting
  4% from slipping
  2% miscellaneous

- The average dollar claims by category are:

Vision	$2,800
Back	2,725
Foot and leg	960
Hearing	681
Hand and arm	592
Stress related	575

SIX-STEP PROBLEM-SOLVING PROCESS (continued)

STEP FOUR: Identify Potential Solutions

Finally, your team enters the long awaited "solution" phase of decision making. The job at hand is to determine possible and recommended solutions to the objective statement of step two. Given the results of the potential causes developed in step three, the team might very well choose to focus initially on possible solutions to back-related injuries caused by lifting.

Many tools will be useful when searching for solutions during this step. For example, cause-and-effect diagrams may act as a solution catalyst. Brainstorming remains a reliable approach also. These and other problem-solving tools are discussed in the latter sections of this book. In this particular case, let's assume the team develops the following table of potential solutions along with dollar-related budgets.

Possible Solution	Costs	Frequency
Redesign work process to eliminate lifting	$210,000	One time
Train workers in proper lifting technique	$ 3,500	Annual
Require all lifting involve two or more individuals	$ 66,200	Annual
Place lifting equipment at all 12 high-incidence locations	$ 69,000	One time
Place lifting equipment at the 4 highest-incident locations	$ 23,000	One time

Based upon their brainstorm analysis, assume the team gained a consensus to recommend that $23,000 be invested to place lifting equipment at the four highest-incident locations for back injuries.

STEP FIVE: Plan and Implement Corrective Action

The identification of potential solutions in step four leads the team to step five: planning and implementing a corrective action plan. Of course, the recommendation would need to be made to the Quality Steering Committee (QSC) and approved since it exceeds the team's budget. If the recommendation were within the team's budgetary authority, it could be implemented on its own. The presentation to the QSC should be well developed and all the team members should be encouraged to attend. Upon approval, the team would recommend a timetable to assist in implementation and suggest a priority of installation. Any training needed would be articulated also, and necessary documentation captured before moving to step six.

STEP SIX: Evaluate and Adjust

It is only natural for a team to feel it has accomplished its objective at the point of implementation. However, a critical evaluation step remains. After the lift equipment has been installed and workers are trained in its use, the team should collect and evaluate data on its action plan. Here the primary question is, ''Did the recommended action meet the objective?'' In this case assume that the lift equipment resulted in a 23 percent reduction in back related workers' compensation claims. Since the objective was to reduce all workers' compensation claims by 30 percent, the team would now return to step two and resume its efforts at continuous improvement. Its final report on the team's effort and any mission clarification should be made with its sponsor at this time.

GETTING GROUP AGREEMENT

The strength of a team is its diversity; it can also be its weakness if disagreement and conflict result in loss of unity. The team makes many decisions (some small, some greater) as it moves toward a recommendation. A key to retaining the positive team aspects is the concept of consensus. Consensus encourages and focuses the team to work together. It also creates equity and ownership in whatever decision is taken. While not every team decision needs consensus, the facilitator should strive for consensus in each step of the problem-solving process and on all major team decisions. If this occurs, greater acceptance and commitment to the decision results.

What Is Consensus?

The road to consensus-building rarely provides a smooth ride. It typically involves investment of time to assure each member's point is heard in a quality manner. It involves collaboration in which each person reviews his or her position in light of others' evidence and experiences, and feels comfortable in retaining or changing his or her position. Consensus is achieved when each individual team member can nod ''yes'' to these types of questions.

► Will you agree this is the next step?

► Can you live with this position?

► Are you comfortable with this course of action?

► Can you support this alternative?

In other words, the *group* can support the position or decision 100 percent even though all members may not totally agree with the position. Consensus is the voluntary giving of consent. Thus it is a win/win situation. It is more valuable than voting since it does not involve a win/lose situation.

HOW DO FACILITATORS GET CONSENSUS?

The facilitator is a key player in assisting team members to reach consensus. To move toward consensus, the facilitator attempts to provide a climate and structure, which includes the following:

- Evaluative criteria are established and revisited.

- Adequate time is given to work through the issue.

- Conflict is perceived as inevitable on the way to consensus.

- Negotiation and collaboration between team members is expected and encouraged to move toward consensus.

- Fact is emphasized over opinion.

- Structured decision-making tools are utilized.

- Giving in on a point is not losing; gaining on an issue is not winning.

- Team members don't give in just to avoid conflict.

- Flipping coins and voting are not viable alternatives to sharing information, debating points, providing data and exploring other alternatives.

Vote Note: The team governance (step one) should address what constitutes agreement within the team. Voting formats are acceptable if the team agrees and uses them selectively rather than routinely.

WHAT IF THE GROUP GETS STUCK?

Regardless of the team tools used and the maturity of team members, occasionally consensus will not be possible. Assuming that the facilitator has given the group adequate time to work through the differences, she might consider any of the following.

► Agree to not agree, and then move to a related issue. If necessary, return to the original issue at a later time.

► Rely on the governance document for voting as an alternative (if established).

► Change topics for a while.

► Call a recess to allow issues to settle; take it back up at the next meeting.

► Work toward a compromise decision knowing it may not be the best decision.

► Rely on team leader's position to make an ''edict'' decision (less desirable).

► Refer item to sponsor group for a decision (less desirable).

Voting to Sort as an Alternative to Consensus

The team members should strive for consensus on major decisions, but often faces what might be called multiple options in movement toward their strategic decisions. For example, in determining causes (step three) or potential solutions (step four) in the problem-solving process, multiple options might be captured by the facilitator as a result of brainstorming or other means. The clustering, sorting and selection of a few ideas can be a cumbersome and time-consuming (as well as frustrating) task. Voting can quickly reduce a large number of options while retaining team commitment.

Multivoting

This technique can be used to reduce an excessive number of items to a more manageable few for further discussion. Thus it is a useful technique to reduce lists quickly without conflict. For example, assume a team's brainstorm has resulted in 25 possible improvements. Since not all of the possible solutions can be pursued, the list needs to be reduced to a more manageable size. On the first vote, the facilitator would give each team member five votes and ask them to vote their five top options on a 3″×5″ card or with a Post-it™ note, which will be taped or stuck on the flip chart. This will typically reduce the original list to less than 10 items. After some discussion, the facilitator would move to a second vote and ask for each team member to vote for their top three options. This will typically result in a list of four to six items. The facilitator can then strive for a consensus through discussion.

Nominal Group Voting

The nominal group technique is a good alternative to multivoting or can be used to further reduce and prioritize the discussion options. Assume that the multivoting exercise (above) resulted in six items remaining and there was not time enough to discuss for consensus. The facilitator then asks each team member to rate the remaining items from ''1'' to ''6'' on a 3″×5″ card or Post-it note. The ''6'' represents the item they most favor and ''1'' the least favored.

These ratings are then tabulated on the flip chart by the facilitator or recorder. The highest scored item represents the team's greatest support. After discussion, the team is asked if it can fully support this item.

THE IMPORTANCE OF PREPARATION

The facilitator is typically responsible for the structure of the team meeting, including room setup, supplies, refreshments, meeting notification and agenda. Carefully planned and prepared meetings greatly enhance the team's productivity; poorly facilitated meetings result in boredom, frustration and indifference.

A successful outcome of a team meeting relies heavily upon what goes on in the meeting. But success also depends upon what happens in preparation for the meeting.

Well over 90 percent of a typical Quality Improvement Team's (QIT) activities take place within a formal meeting structure.

Meeting Notification and Agenda

Meeting notifications are simple but essential tools for effective meetings. The team notification should be developed and distributed in a timely manner and should include essential meeting information, a meeting objective and an agenda.

While the meeting information is self-explanatory, facilitators are urged to make use of the coordinating instructions for better utilization of time.

When the agenda is part of the meeting notification, the restatement of the overall team objective as well as the specific meeting objective aids in focusing the team effort. Obviously, the agenda items support the meeting objective. Generally, times are illustrated next to agenda items. This indication of time is a good organizational device as long as team members understand the meeting is to be "value driven" and not "time" driven. In other words, if progress is being made, don't fret about meeting each agenda item's time allocation. In fact, ask this question at meetings: "Are we making progress?" rather than, "Did we cover all agenda items?" However, *meeting ending times are sacred.* Note ending time on the agenda and always end on or before that time.

A sample meeting notification incorporating objective statements and agenda is illustrated below for a Safety QIT involved in the reduction of workers' compensation claims due to injury. Note this might be an agenda in step three of the team problem-solving process.

> **Tip:** Regardless of the agenda, attempt to get involvement from the team members within the first five minutes. This creates an environment of participation that carries over throughout the meeting.

Sample Meeting Notification and Agenda

To:　　　Safety QIT members (Childers, Graff, Lutz, Gomez, Chung, Brown)

From:　　Margaret Graham, Box 12, ext. 3118

Subject:　Safety QIT meeting notification

The weekly Safety QIT meeting notification and agenda are as follows. If you cannot attend, please let me know by Tuesday, February 9.

When:　Friday, February 12
Where:　Conference Room B
Time:　3:30–4:45 P.M.

Coordinating Instructions:

Childers and Brown to bring claims information.

Gomez and Lutz are to bring pocket calculators, legal pads and pens.

AGENDA

Team Objective:　To reduce workers' compensation claims by 30 percent during the next 18 months.

Meeting Objective:　To sort workers' compensation claims of the last 36 months according to injury category and average dollar size.

Topic	*Time*
1. Review and revision of agenda and objective	5 minutes
2. Report on minutes, last meeting	10 minutes
3. Sorting of claims by injury category and frequency	50 minutes
4. Review of meeting actions	5 minutes
5. Inputs for next meeting agenda	5 minutes

Distribution: Brown, Childers, Chung, Gomez, Graff, Lutz

RUNNING AN EFFECTIVE TEAM MEETING

As a facilitator, ensure that the five major causes of poor meetings are eliminated from your team meetings and you will find greater productivity and satisfaction in team gatherings.

CAUSES	WHAT TO DO
Late-starting meetings	As facilitator, arrive early and get organized. Be assertive and start on time! If meetings begin late, the tardy participants are rewarded and on-time participants are penalized. Obviously, late-starting meetings are also unproductive.
Wandering from agenda and tendencies to gripe	Tactfully refocus the group back to the agenda purpose and agenda item.
Failure to set and end meetings on time	Always indicate ending time on meeting notification and always end meetings at designated time.
Lack of summary	Summarize the action or decision after each agenda item and summarize again at end of meeting. Also indicate time frames and responsibilities for each action item to provide reminders and reinforcement.
Lack of minutes	Use your flip chart sheets as minutes. Take five minutes to record selectively major actions, decisions and assignments. Distribute to team members in a timely manner.

MANAGING THE MEETING'S PHYSICAL ENVIRONMENT

If team members are not comfortable, they will not focus as effectively on the meeting objective. Irritations within the physical environment include personal discomfort due to inappropriate temperature, noise, lighting, seating or ventilation. Dirty or untidy rooms can also be bothersome, as are insufficient supplies, missing or broken equipment, or a poor location or view.

The room arrangement—including furniture and equipment setup—are essential to group effectiveness. However the ideal arrangement may vary from meeting to meeting. For example, if the team is going to work as a group, with plenty of documentation, a large table is necessary. If the team will be brainstorming, a writing surface is not as essential. Therefore, feel comfortable changing the room setup to fulfill the meeting objective.

Noted below are several desirable configurations for a group meeting using facilitation and team involvement. Also shown are some configurations that are not so feasible. Note that in each case, the preferred arrangement focuses on the issues and group memory as captured on a flip chart or other surface. The key principle is to keep a focus on issues—not on individuals—while encouraging team involvement and comfort.

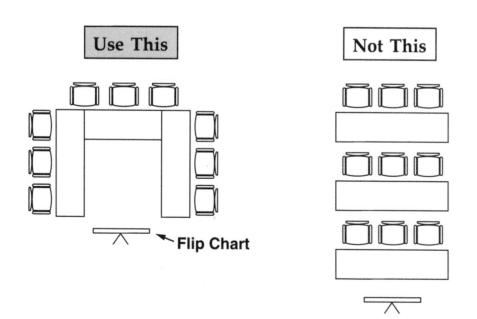

MANAGING THE MEETING'S PHYSICAL ENVIRONMENT (continued)

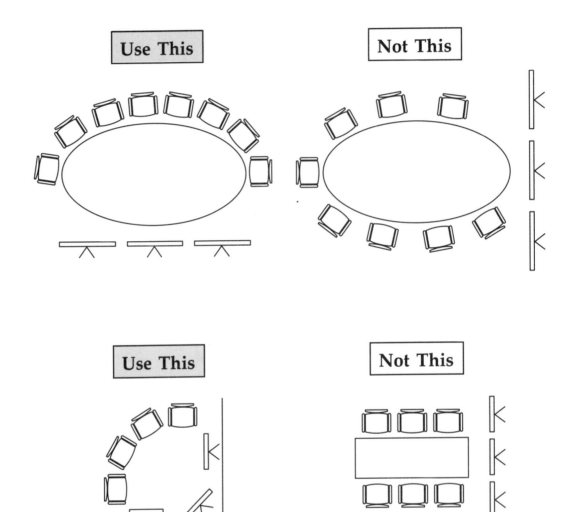

Check it off! Use the accompanying checklist to make sure you haven't forgotten any meeting details.

Team Meeting Checklist

MEETING ROOM

- ☐ Room reservation made
- ☐ Room available for early set-up
- ☐ Permission granted for taping pages to wall
- ☐ Wall space for taping flip chart pages
- ☐ Room is climate controlled
- ☐ Room is clean
- ☐ Adequate lighting available
- ☐ Adequate and appropriate tables and chairs
- ☐ Plans made for proper furniture setup
- ☐ Break-out rooms/space for subgroups
- ☐ Other: _____

PRENOTIFICATION AND AGENDA

- ☐ Prenotification distributed in timely and accurate manner
- ☐ Arrangements made for guests
- ☐ Meeting objective clearly stated
- ☐ Agenda distributed prior to meeting
- ☐ Advance material distributed
- ☐ Coordinating instructions included
- ☐ Copies of minutes from last meeting available
- ☐ Other: _____

Team Meeting Checklist **(continued)**

SUPPLIES AND EQUIPMENT

☐ Adequate easels and flip-chart pads

☐ Masking tape, pins or thumb tacks

☐ Post-it™ note pads

☐ Set of pens (four colors)

☐ Participant note pads and pens

☐ Other: _____

MISCELLANEOUS

☐ Refreshments available

☐ Proper signage to room

☐ Name tags or tents for initial meeting

☐ Washrooms location known, and indicated to participants

☐ Break times indicated to participants

☐ Other: _____

TEAM LIFE CYCLES

A team evolves through a life cycle from birth to maturity. Each stage of the cycle has predictable transition characteristics. The facilitator who knows what to expect in these stages is better prepared to serve the members' needs and help team members deal with the situations inherent in each stage.

Jack Orsburn and his colleagues have characterized the predictable stages in team development.* Below are the team characteristics for each stage.

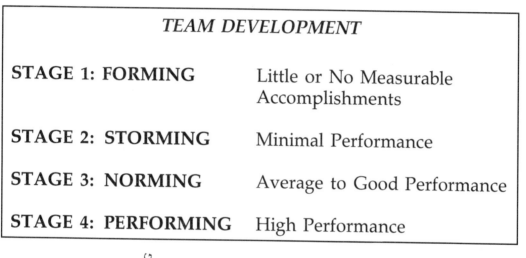

TEAM DEVELOPMENT	
STAGE 1: FORMING	Little or No Measurable Accomplishments
STAGE 2: STORMING	Minimal Performance
STAGE 3: NORMING	Average to Good Performance
STAGE 4: PERFORMING	High Performance

* Partially adapted from *Self-Directed Work Teams*, by Jack Orsburn, Linda Moran, Ed Musselwhite, and John Zenger. Published by Business One Irwin, 1990.

TEAM LIFE CYCLES (continued)

STAGE 1: FORMING

The forming stage represents the movement of an individual into the group-member status. Most team members will greatly anticipate their involvement. The team members' characteristics and suggested facilitator actions of this "feeling out" stage include:

Team Member Characteristics:

- Hesitant participation tempered with optimism

- Organizational complaints and gripes common

- Some suspicion and fear of team situation

- Looking for sense of belonging

- Closely watching other team members' behaviors

Facilitator Behaviors:

- Ensure team members get acquainted

- Be sensitive to team members' needs

- Provide clear direction and information

- Give team simple tasks

- Provide intensive "awareness" training

- Provide training on team-building tools

STAGE 2: STORMING

Although a layperson would expect progress to pick up during this stage, little actually develops. In fact, this stage has great downside possibilities if the facilitator does not effectively counter these tendencies.

Team Member Characteristics:

- Conflict between team members begins to show

- "One-upmanship" develops

- Concern over team versus individual responsibilities

- Continuing confusion about team members' roles

Facilitator Behaviors:

- Continue to be positive and informative

- Reassure team that current conflict is normal

- Deal openly with conflict

- Give team more responsible tasks

- Continue to train on team building and team tools

TEAM LIFE CYCLES (continued)

STAGE 3: NORMING

In this stage the team begins to come together. Conflict is substantially reduced as the team grows in confidence and begins to find that the team concept is working.

Team Member Characteristics:

- Over-reliance on team leader/facilitator possible

- Conflicts reduced among team members

- Sharing and discussing become team norms

- Greater team cohesiveness develops

- Harmony among team members becomes common

Facilitator Behaviors:

- Provide less structure as team matures

- Give team even more responsibility

- Ensure team does not overly rely on any one member

- Continue to provide team development and training opportunities

STAGE 4: PERFORMING

As maturity continues, *team* behavior becomes the norm. While team members may be occasionally replaced, the team has become self-functioning. The team routinely defines and solves more difficult issues.

Team Member Characteristics:

- Intense loyalty among team members develops

- Teams may mask individual dysfunctional members

- Teams can become competitive with other teams

- Teams need greater information

- Teams become more innovative

- Team members become more confident

Facilitator Behaviors:

- Ensure team's information needs are fulfilled

- Ensure that the team celebrates its successes

- Encourage team toward continued growth

- Continue to train; ensure new team members are properly trained

- Encourage team members to rotate roles

- Reduce your involvement as team grows

- Continue to foster trust and commitment among team members

Team Development Exercise

Identify the following sentences relating to team development stages by placing an F (Forming), S (Storming), N (Norming), or P (Performing) in the space provided. Check your answers with those in the box at the bottom of the page.

_____ **1.** Conflict between team members begins to show.

_____ **2.** Looking for a sense of belonging.

_____ **3.** Organizational complaints and gripes are common.

_____ **4.** Harmony among team members becomes common.

_____ **5.** Teams need greater information.

_____ **6.** Intense loyalty among team members develops.

_____ **7.** "One-upsmanship" develops.

_____ **8.** Sharing and discussing become team norms.

_____ **9.** Teams can become competitive with other teams.

_____ **10.** Some suspicion and fear of team situation.

_____ **11.** Concern over team versus individual responsibilities develops.

_____ **12.** Over-reliance on facilitator possible.

Answers: 1. S   2. F   3. F   4. N   5. P   6. P   7. S   8. N   9. P   10. F   11. S   12. N

HANDLING DIFFICULT TEAM MEMBERS

The question most frequently asked by newly appointed facilitators is how to handle troublesome team members. A companion question is when to confront a troublesome participant.

WHEN to Handle a Difficult Team Member

A participant is designated as troublesome when his or her behavior is directly and negatively impacting the team's productivity or hindering the team's cohesiveness in terms of openness, trust, commitment and participation.

Most facilitators become alarmed too early about team members' conduct and label some as troublesome. Generally, a facilitator should not be too concerned about individuals' conduct within the first four to six months of team formation, especially if the undesirable behaviors occur only occasionally. This initial period may be quite different from later meetings, given the considerable amount of transition that may be taking place.

If the behavior does not subside in an appropriate time period, or is of a severe nature, the facilitator or team leader should take action to address the troublesome member's conduct.

HANDLING DIFFICULT TEAM MEMBERS (continued)

HOW to Handle a Troublesome Team Member

In working with this individual, your goal is to reduce, alter or eliminate the member's undesirable behaviors without hurting his self-esteem or capability to contribute. Thus, you should never verbally scold or embarass the individual in front of the group or even privately.

Your first opportunity to correct troublesome behavior should be during the meeting. If an individual is dominating the discussion, try, ''Helen, you have made several contributions; I want to hear how other group members see this issue.'' The key is to be direct, but tactful.

A second option is to talk with the person candidly about the behavior in private. For example, if a person is rarely contributing to the discussion, you might approach the team member before the meeting and say, ''Chuck, I really need your input on this issue; is there some reason you aren't contributing?''

A third option is to use the team's informal leaders—those members most respected for their knowledge and experience. These ''leaders'' can help if you ask them to tactfully intervene. Finally, you may wish periodically to ask the team to self-analyze their development and to bring negative team behaviors to the surface for discussion.

Listed on the next pages are four of the most frequently encountered types of troublesome team members that hamper group growth. Additional facilitator tips to modify their behaviors are included also.

MUMMY
WINDBAG
RAMBLER
HOMESTEADER

NO. I DON'T KNOW . . .

I DO! I'VE DONE THE . . .

YES, I SEE YOUR POINT. . . . DID I TELL YOU ABOUT THE SOLUTION WE APPLIED WHEN . . .

I DON'T SEE THE POINT IN PURSUING THIS ANY FURTHER WHEN MY SOLUTION IS SO OBVIOUS!

| **The Mummy** | This person will not freely participate in discussions. The motivation might be indifference, an inferiority complex, confusion about the issues or process, or a feeling of superiority. |

Facilitator Antidotes:

- Be patient.

- Use a warm-up exercise; give the Mummy a major role.

- Ask direct questions to the person on topics you know he or she has expertise.

- Assign these people as subgroup facilitators.

- Ask this member if you can help clarify the process or if someone in the group can help clarify the issues.

| **The Windbag** | This individual comments too frequently and tends to dominate discussions. He or she also tends to be the first to speak on each issue. |

Facilitator Antidotes:

- Establish procedures to limit the Windbag's discussion, e.g., ''Each of you has a nickel and that represents only five minutes of remarks on this issue.''

- Target questions to other members by name.

- Use nonverbal signals, e.g., no direct eye contact, focus on another part of meeting room.

- Do not assign subgroup leadership roles to this person.

HANDLING DIFFICULT TEAM MEMBERS (continued)

| The Rambler | This individual will often get off track in his remarks and uses low-probability exceptions or far-fetched examples to make a point.

Facilitator Antidotes:

- Preface the Rambler's remarks with, ''Bill, because of time constraints, give me your short version—twenty words or less.''

- When he pauses, say ''Thanks Bill, but we do need to get back to the agenda.''

- Do not assign a subgroup leadership role to this person.

- Consider making this individual a recorder, thus neutralizing his remarks.

| The Homesteader | A person who takes an initial position and is highly reluctant to budge or consider other viable alternatives.

Facilitator Antidotes:

- Apply ''hints'' on consensus building.

- Overwhelm with facts.

- Enlist support of team members.

- Give the Homesteader a graceful way out with an alternative.

A Comment About Reluctant Team Members

An often-asked question is what to do about employees who do not want to be on a team. We advise that you not force involvement, but rather allow the dynamics of the team process and the excitement of other team members to arouse their interest and motivate them to fully participate in the team concept.

QUIZ: THE MATCH GAME

Match facilitator antidotes listed on the left with the troublesome team member type listed on the right. Answers may be used more than once. Answers are at the bottom of the page.

_____ 1. Target questions to other members by name

a. Mummy

_____ 2. Overwhelm with facts

b. Windbag

_____ 3. Assign these people as sub-group facilitators

c. Rambler

_____ 4. Do not assign a subgroup leadership role to this person

d. Homesteader

_____ 5. Enlist support of team members

_____ 6. Be patient

_____ 7. Consider making this person a recorder, thus neutralizing remarks

_____ 8. When person pauses, thank them and remind them of need to stick to the agenda

Answers: 1. b 2. d 3. a 4. b or c 5. d 6. a 7. c 8. c

WHAT IF THE GROUP STILL GETS STUCK?

The aim of this entire book is to provide guidance on how a facilitator can effectively move a group toward its goal. At times even the effective use of structure, tools and skills will not keep a team from getting bogged down. Realize this is predictable and natural. When this occurs, the facilitator can often assist. First, the facilitator needs to try to determine the cause of this dilemma. Do they lack the tools and knowledge to go forward? Have they become too dependent on you or the team leader for movement or are they simply in conflict and having trouble collaborating?

Next acknowledge and get agreement from participants that the team is stuck; then, ensure that all participants agree to the specific objective and task to which the group committed. If you are off track, get agreement to move back to the agenda.

Sometimes the group members will be involved with too much detail. If so, suggest they move to a broader issue. At other times participants will become bogged down in gripe sessions and point out how organizational policy contradicts their solutions. When this happens, encourage the team to keep its focus and not deal with issues that are bigger than their objective or beyond their control. Most importantly, encourage the team to continue in collaborative behavior to move through this period.

Other Resources

Teams sometimes get stuck when they believe they must develop answers solely within their group. To avoid falling into this trap, the facilitator should encourage the group to seek outside assistance on a routine basis. Some measures that will re-energize the members include:

- ▶ Visiting other firms with similar situations; visiting customers
- ▶ Calling the trade association for assistance
- ▶ Seeking assistance from governmental or regulatory agencies
- ▶ Inviting other organizational members with expertise
- ▶ Asking in outside experts
- ▶ Seeking assistance from suppliers or vendors
- ▶ Reviewing library or trade literature on the topic
- ▶ Checking corporate records (maybe the same problem was creatively addressed 30 years ago).

P A R T

III

Facilitation Tools

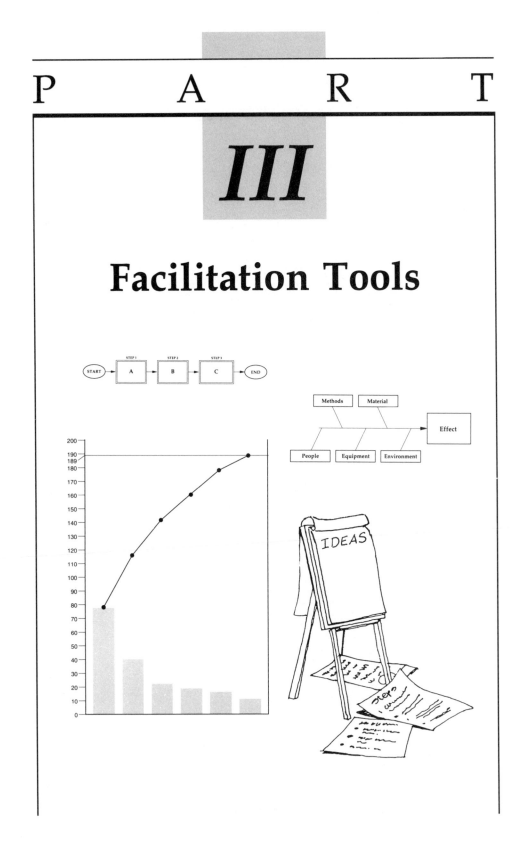

ESSENTIAL TOOLS

A team that is involved in improving quality needs tools to use in identifying causes of and potential solutions to problems and issues. Recall that the facilitator is responsible for the meeting structure, and therefore, the timely and effective use of these tools by the team. Additionally, it is often the facilitator's responsibility to provide initial or refresher training on these tools. Four of the most frequently used team tools are flowcharts, brainstorming, cause-and-effect (fishbone) diagrams, and Pareto diagrams.

Process Flowcharts

Before team members can identify causes or make improvement suggestions, they must understand what the system or process involves. Recall that a process is simply a sequentially connected set of events with an outcome. The flowchart helps to ensure that members understand the steps in the process by documenting in proper sequence the flow of paper, information, product or material.

Once these steps are documented, the team can analyze the steps with the aim of eliminating, combining, simplifying, or otherwise modifying the process.

ESSENTIAL TOOLS (continued)

Flowchart Symbols

To construct a flowchart, team members must first understand the most common symbols.

Double rectangles indicate the primary steps in the process. All other symbols and flows are derived from these steps.

The oval indicates the beginning or end of a process. The word "start" or "end" is written inside the symbol.

An arrow indicates the movement and direction of information, paper, material or product within the process.

The rectangle indicates an activity not involving a decision. The activity is noted inside the symbol. One or more arrows can be shown flowing into a rectangle, but only one arrow can leave the symbol.

The diamond is used to indicate alternatives or decisions that are noted inside the symbol. Only one arrow can flow into a decision symbol; two or more arrows may flow out.

The exaggerated capital "D" indicates a delay or hold in the process flow. The reason for the delay is indicated inside the symbol.

How to Construct a Flowchart

There are three major steps to follow in the construction of a flowchart:

STEP 1. Develop major steps

STEP 2. List substeps for each major step

STEP 3. Identify flowchart symbols and complete the flowchart

Let's examine each of these steps in greater detail using an example of a telephone-registration process.

STEP 1: Developing Major Steps

Assume that you are a member of a Quality Improvement Team (QIT) charged with improving the telephone-registration process in a management training organization. The organization promotes its seminars through direct mail brochures distributed in their market area. Customers then call or mail in their registrations. They are processed and subsequently the customers are mailed program confirmation letters. Thus the major steps in the telephone registration might be flowcharted as illustrated.

HOW TO CONSTRUCT A FLOWCHART
(continued)

STEP 2: List Substeps for Each Major Step

After the major steps are identified, the team identifies the steps involved within the boundaries of each major step. For example, the listing of substeps might be:

Major Step: **Telephone Registration Received by Receptionist**

Substeps:
- Customer information filled in on enrollment form
- Check to see if customer qualifies for discount
- Place enrollment card in registrar's ''in'' box for processing

Major Step: **Registrar Processes Customer Reservation**

Substeps:
- Registrar inputs registration into computer
- Runs check to determine customer's account is in good standing
- Prints confirmation letter to customer
- Address of confirmation letter checked for special instructions (i.e., to individual or to Human Resource Director, duplicate copies, etc.)

Major Step: **Mail clerk prepares and mails confirmation letters**

Substeps:
- Confirmation letters printed
- Letters folded by assistant and stuffed in envelopes on same day received
- Any special actions communicated back to registrar for input into customer file
- Distribution and mailing of confirmation letters

Hint: The facilitator may want to prepare a taped separate flip chart sheet for each major step on the wall and have recorder list substeps using flip chart on easel, then tape the substeps to that major step sheet.

STEP 3: Identify Flowchart Symbols and Complete the Flowchart

Lastly, after you have defined all the substeps, choose the appropriate flowchart symbol for each step and construct the chart noting the action or activity within each step. A complete flowchart for the telephone process is shown on page 72.

After Flowcharting: Identifying Process Improvement Options

A finished flowchart provides a valuable visual representation of the registration process, enabling the team to more clearly identify alternative ways to improve the process. For example, should any decision points or steps be eliminated or can any steps be eliminated, reduced, simplified or otherwise modified to improve efficiency and quality? Can any activities be eliminted? Can any delays be reduced? Here are a few possibilities the team might identify for further consideration:

► Can registration data be directly entered into the computer, thus eliminating the registration form tasks?

► Could all registration calls be directly forwarded to the registrar, thus eliminating the first major step?

► Could steps in confirmation mailing be further automated?

► Could delays in in-boxes be reduced?

FLOWCHART EXAMPLE

Flowchart of Telephone-Registration Process

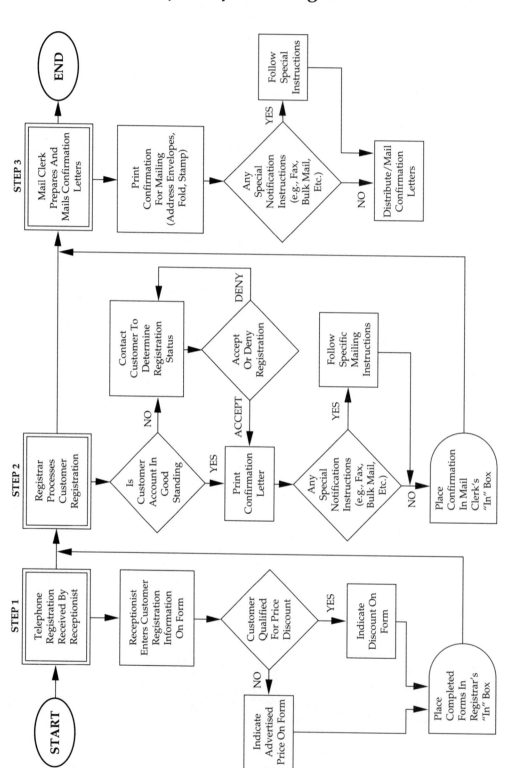

CUSTOMER CONSIDERATIONS

Remembering that it is the customer who ultimately defines and evaluates the quality of a product or service, it is useful to examine the flowcharted process from the customer's perspective. Customers of service businesses in particular may play many different roles in the process and have unique vantage points that should not be overlooked. Here are three customer functions that are particularly relevant:

✔ *Interaction* with employees, e.g., to place an order, to request information

✔ *Waiting* before, during, or after service, e.g., waiting for a table at a restaurant, waiting for food to be prepared, waiting to pay the cashier after the meal

✔ *Active participation* in the creation of the service, e.g., preparing salad at a restaurant's salad bar, pumping gasoline at a self-service gas station, or finding the needed merchandise at a retail store

To analyze the service flowchart from the customer's perspective, ask questions such as: Can the quality of the interaction between the employee and customer be improved? Can unnecessary waits be eliminated? Can the customer be made to feel more comfortable during unavoidable waiting periods? Is the customer willing and able to play his role as an active participant in creating the service? How can the process be made more convenient for the customer? And so on.

UNSCRAMBLING THE MESS: A FLOWCHARTING EXERCISE

Are you ready to test your flowcharting skills? If so, construct a flowchart using the following activities, decisions, and alternatives that a front-counter employee at a fast-food restaurant might follow in processing a customer's order. Based upon the 23 steps and substeps that are listed in random order, your finished flowchart should include three double rectangles, thirteen other rectangles, three diamonds, two "Ds," and two ovals. As a hint, let the first three items in the list represent the major steps.

- Greet the customer
- Fill order
- Complete transaction
- Gather napkins and other condiments for customer
- Hand ordered items to customer
- Ring order on cash register
- Say "good morning" and solicit customer's order
- Place all items on tray or in paper bag
- Has the customer paid with correct change?
- Is the order dine-in or carry out?
- Fill drink portion of order while food is processed
- Collect payment from customer
- End
- Thank customer
- Record ordered items on notepad
- Start
- Route order to cooks
- Place tray on counter for order
- Place opened paper bag on counter
- Assemble ordered food items
- Any special requests by customer?
- Make change as necessary
- Make sure special requests are honored (e.g., extra catsup)

When you have finished drawing the flowchart, compare yours with the authors' version on page 90.

FACILITATING BRAINSTORMING

Another proven problem-solving tool is brainstorming. Facilitators use this technique to develop a "storm" of ideas in a structured format. It is most heavily used in steps 3 through 5 of the problem-solving steps. Brainstorms are most effective with groups ranging from three to eight people.

Brainstorming is effective as both a problem-solving tool and as a team builder. The team building benefits are derived from equal opportunity for participation from each team member and the subsequent trust developed from that involvement. The problem-solving value derives from the creativity and idea generation of different perspectives.

Brainstorm Guidelines

The facilitator or recorder typically uses the flip chart and flip-chart techniques to record the brainstorm responses and begins by stating, "Let's brainstorm."

☐ Clearly state the purpose, topic, issue and guidelines for the brainstorm.

☐ Set a distinct period of time for the brainstorm, i.e., 12 to 20 minutes.

☐ Each team member, in sequence, makes a contribution. (Encourage team members' ideas even if they seem "far out" or ridiculous.)

☐ Allow no evaluations, criticisms, comments or discussions during the generation of ideas. (Comments might cause people to censor their ideas or otherwise dampen the creative process.)

☐ "Passing their turn" by team members with continued participation is allowed. (Quantity of ideas is a goal of this technique.)

☐ Piggybacking, i.e. building on others' ideas is encouraged without the barrier of "pride of ownership." (If a number of participants pass, the facilitator might open the session up to "greenlighting," whereby all members can contribute ideas without waiting for their turn.

☐ When all team members have passed, the facilitator asks, "Are we through?"

WORKSHEET: WORKER INJURY CAUSES

To illustrate, a team's brainstorming worksheet on the possible causes of worker injuries might look like this:

CAUSES OF INJURY

- bulky material
- raw material too heavy
- material prone to shatter
- difficult-to-grip materials
- improper technique
- taking shortcuts
- rushing by employees
- carelessness by employees
- tables too high
- unsafe shoes
- improper safety shield
- worn-out drill
- slippery footing
- lack of safety rules
- repetitive actions
- lack of training
- too much overtime
- overlooking safety rules
- supervisors expect too much
- supervisors overlook safety policy
- lack of lifting equipment
- poor lighting
- limited signage

Facilitator Closure On Brainstorming

During the actual brainstorming, the facilitator has acted primarily as a recorder with only brief moments of participation to clarify ideas.

After the ideas have been generated, the facilitator moves into a more traditional role to reduce the idea list to a more manageable size. Questioning, multivoting, and nominal group techniques can be used to gain consensus on the ideas to be further developed. Brainstorming ideas are often used as the basis for another team tool called cause-and-effect diagrams.

CAUSE-AND-EFFECT DIAGRAMS

Brainstorming, document analysis, or some other means often provide the team with many potential causes or solutions to an issue.

To provide greater structure for the team in their analysis, a cause-and-effect diagram often helps by further subgrouping the issue under major headings. One common form of a cause-and-effect diagram is called the ''fishbone diagram.'' Three steps are involved in constructing a fishbone.

STEP ONE: Construct Effect

The fishbone diagram is constructed by identifying the team's problem or specific issue in a rectangle. This box represents the effect and is alluded to as the fish head. For example, in our safety issue noted earlier, the effect concerns workers' compensation claims. Illustrated below, an arrow represents the ''fish spine'' that connects the causes to the effect.

STEP TWO: Add Subgroups

Most causes to an organizational issue can be grouped under the headings of material, equipment, people, methods, or environment. These cause subgroups represent the ''bones'' of the fishbone diagram.

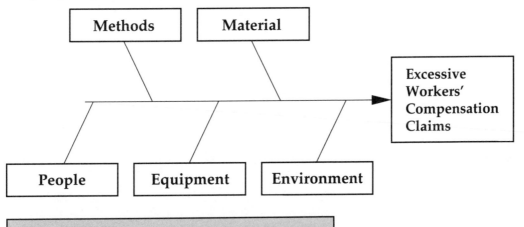

STEP THREE: Add Potential Causes

The last step is to add the brainstorm ideas to the subgroups as additional branches stemming from these groups. As an exercise, place the possible causes of injuries derived from the team brainstorm (page 76) as branches on the fishbone chart. Note that with additional ''bones'' you are attempting to sort further on common-denominator criteria. Check your cause-and-effect diagrams with the figure below. Once the fishbone diagram is completed as shown, the team is able to more effectively discuss possible solutions to remedy each problem or likely cause.

Completed Fishbone Diagram

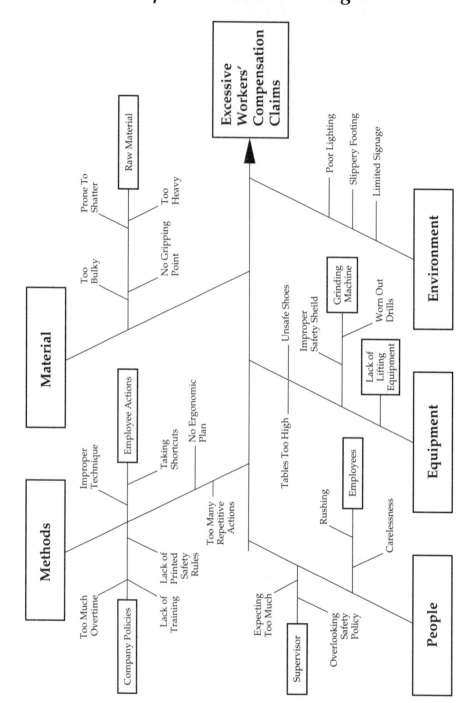

PARETO DIAGRAMS

While studying the distribution of Italian wealth in the 1800s, economist Vilfredo Pareto found that 20 percent of the families held 80 percent of the wealth. Similar distributions were observed elsewhere until the phenomena eventually became known as the 80–20 principle. This phenomenon of the "critical few" can be applied to many of the quality issues that work teams face. For example, other manifestations of the Pareto effect are:

✔ About 20% of our employees account for 80% of absences.

✔ About 20% of quality issues account for 80% of quality mistakes.

✔ About 20% of our products account for 80% of our revenues.

The Pareto principle is used to differentiate the most critical causes from the many potential causes in a quality issue. Revisiting the statistics used by the QIT Safety Team provides an example of how a Pareto diagram might be constructed and used.

Constructing a Pareto Diagram

To construct a Pareto diagram, begin with a bar graph placing injury categories (identified by the work team), on the horizontal axis. In the example shown below, the data are plotted from the original data taken from the worksheet first illustrated on page 76. Note that the bars in the example are arranged in descending order, with the back injury shown at the far left. These categories are plotted according to the left vertical axis illustrating the number or frequency of injuries. This vertical axis should extend enough to account for the total injuries recorded, i.e., 103 in our example.

Pareto Diagram of Factory Floor Injury Data

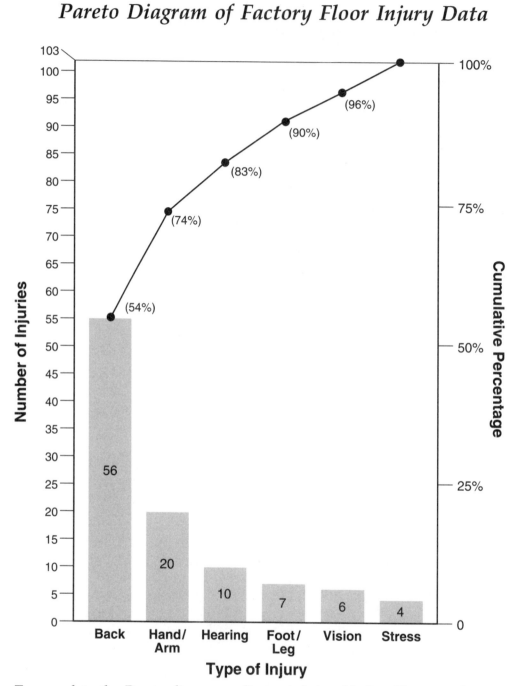

To complete the Pareto diagram, a line graph is added to illustrate the cumulative percentage of factory floor injuries. To plot this, note the following worksheet. A cumulative frequency column is developed of the factory floor injuries. This is developed by adding back injury totals to the "hand and arm" total, i.e., 56 + 20 = 76. Then add the hearing injury data to that cumulative total, 10 + 76 = 86. The last cumulative frequency column number will equal the total number of injuries, i.e., 103.

The cumulative frequency column is then used to develop the cumulative percentages for each injury. Cumulative percentage is developed by dividing the cumulative frequency by the total injuries and multiplying by 100 percent. Example for back injury is as follows:

$$\frac{\text{Cumulative Frequency}}{\text{Total Injuries}} \times 100\% \text{ or } {}^{56}/_{103} \times 100\% = 54$$

The last step is to construct a second vertical axis on the right side of the diagram and label it cumulative percentage. Plot the cumulative percentage values against this axis and make a graph.

WORKSHEET: FACTORY FLOOR INJURY DATA			
Category	Injury Frequency	Cumulative Frequency	Cumulative Percentage
Back Injury	56	56	54
Hand & Arm	20	76	74
Hearing	10	86	83
Foot & Leg	7	93	90
Vision	6	99	96
Stress	4	103	100
Total Injuries	103		

Pareto diagram analysis visually alerts the team of the extent to which the "critical few" phenomenon is present in their process improvement analysis. If one category represents a disproportionate amount of the data—as it does in this example—the Pareto effect is present. The team now knows that focusing on reduction of back injuries will pay the greatest returns in accident reduction.

As a final point, remember that choosing the categories for analysis is critical. For example, in this situation, the team plotted type of injury according to frequency without regard to dollar amount. However, if back injuries resulted in modest dollar losses per injury and eye injuries involved extremely large losses per injury, then the diagrams would not give a complete picture. Also, if back injuries involved only a few lost work days, whereas stress related injuries averaged several weeks of lost time, an incomplete analysis would be shown. In these cases, a Pareto diagram based upon dollar loss or days lost might be more appropriate.

PARETO EXERCISE

Suppose your team was concerned about absenteeism throughout the plant. Draw a Pareto diagram using the following data obtained from each department.

Absentee Data	
Department	Absentee Days (per 1,000 scheduled worker days, during past 12 months)
A	17
B	41
C	78
D	23
E	11
F	19

Your Pareto Diagram

When completed, compare your Pareto diagram with the one shown below.

Pareto Diagram of Sample Absentee Data

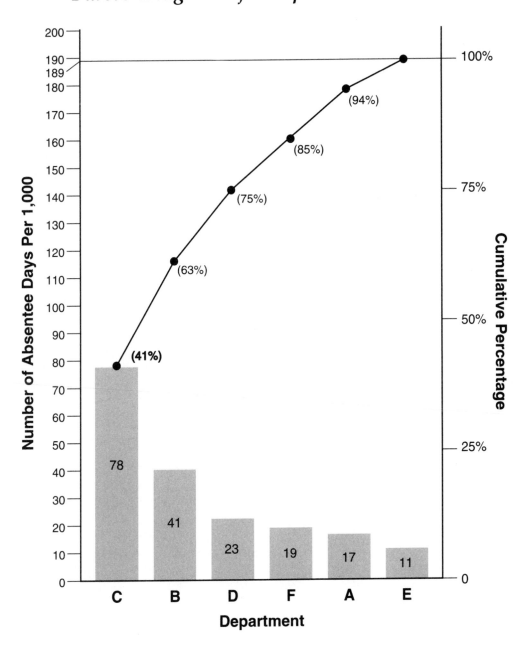

CONCLUSION

Effective work teams do not just happen. Assembled groups of individuals become productive teams only when there is a commitment to the facilitative process. And the process—as should be obvious by this concluding section of the book—requires organization, planning, and a multitude of skills.

An effective facilitator is more than a discussion leader. He or she encourages all team members to participate and helps to focus the team's discussion to solve challenging problems. Consequently, a number of communication and interpersonal skills come into play, involving nonverbal messages as well as an array of questioning techniques.

A keen awareness of the decision-making process is another characteristic of effective team leaders. This process begins by verifying the team's charter and establishing rules of governance. The team objective is then clarified, followed by probing efforts to identify the root or major cause of the problem. When a consensus is reached as to the nature of the problem, the skillful facilitator must then lead the team as it identifies possible solutions and develops a plan to implement the solutions. Finally, the facilitator may assist in the control of the plan, i.e., the evaluation of the plan's implementation for the purpose of possible corrective action. The skillful use of specific problem-solving tools such as flowcharts, brainstorming, cause-and-effect diagrams, and Pareto diagrams enables the facilitator to focus the team's efforts and guide the team through the decision-making process.

Throughout the planning process, skillful facilitators must navigate the sometimes turbulent waters of group dynamics. Building a consensus among team members can be difficult at times, as can dealing with troublesome team members. Facilitators must be sensitive to the individual personalities, thought processes, conversation styles, and strengths that each member brings to the team.

As a planner, the effective facilitator also plans the meeting by attending to numerous details. Notifying team members of meetings, preparing an agenda, arranging the meeting room, and making sure all necessary materials are readily available are just a few of the planning details.

Clearly, effective facilitation can be a challenge, as can be the process of remembering the myriad of terms, concepts, and tools leading to this final section in the book. As a final exercise, test your memory of your new vocabulary by filling in the crossword puzzle on page 87. Give yourself an extra pat on the back if you can complete it *before* checking your answers on page 91.

Happy facilitating!

P A R T

IV

Crossword
Facilitation

EXERCISE: TEST YOUR MEMORY

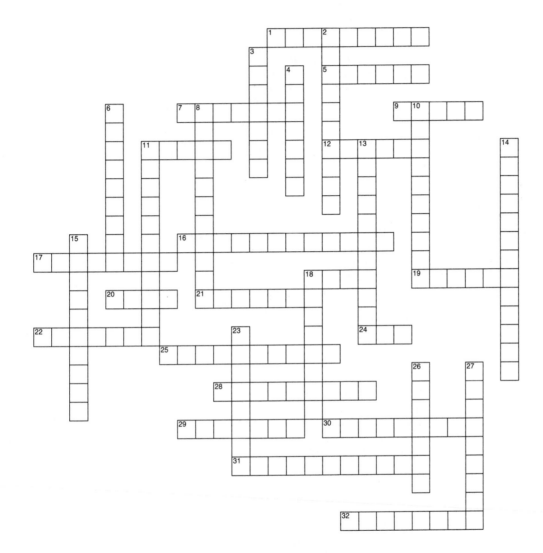

Turn to pages 88 and 89 for clues to "across" and "down."

CROSSWORD CLUES

ACROSS

1. We communicate with these both verbally and nonverbally.

5. A leader "sees" this when others might not.

7. This is specified before the team forms.

9. _____ ended questions tend to elicit responses that are too short for discussion purposes.

11. This troublesome team member might have an inferiority complex.

12. Document that helps keep team discussions focused.

16. What this book is all about!

17. An effective facilitator might use this to generate a discussion.

18. Together everyone accomplishes more.

19. Sometimes referred to as 80–20.

20. This chart helps to record meeting minutes.

21. This person may not want to follow #12 across.

22. Greater team cohesiveness and harmony develop when teams are in this stage of development.

24. Movement that has given rise to increased number of work teams.

25. Communication is largely one-way.

28. Preferable to taking a vote.

29. This type of troublesome team member may try to dominate the discussion.

30. A key role of the facilitator is to clarify and manage this.

31. Facilitators should use this questioning technique when they are asked questions pertaining to content.

32. A diagnostic technique to help the team understand what factors give rise to the apparent "problem."

DOWN

2. A set of rules under which the team operates.

3. Atittudes, values, beliefs, and behavior of a group of people.

4. The team may accomplish very little in this stage.

6. This tool helps team members to understand the sequence of a process.

8. This team member may be reluctant to consider viable alternatives other than his own.

10. Authoritarian styles of this do not make for effective facilitation.

11. Quickly reduces longer lists of alternatives to shorter ones.

13. Addressing this set of issues in planning the meeting helps team members to feel physically comfortable.

14. Several ideas may be generated quickly.

15. Teams doing this are mature and effective.

18. During this process the instructor may ask questions to evaluate learning.

23. A team member greatly assists the facilitator in this role.

26. This domain is beyond the scope of the facilitator's role.

27. Represents a further refinement of the team mission.

Example of Fast-Food Flowchart

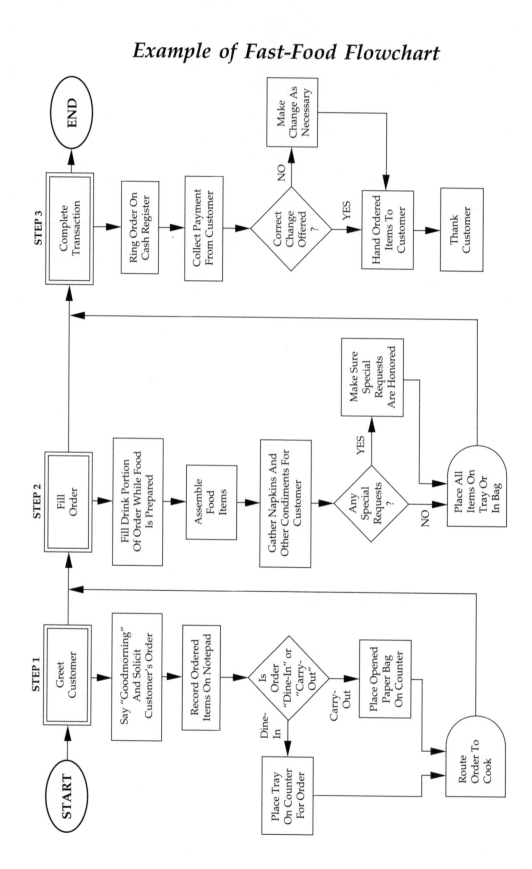

CROSSWORD PUZZLE SOLUTION

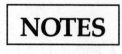

NOTES

NOTES

NOTES

OVER 150 BOOKS AND 35 VIDEOS AVAILABLE IN THE 50-MINUTE SERIES

We hope you enjoyed this book. If so, we have good news for you. This title is part of the best-selling *50-MINUTE*™ *Series* of books. All *Series* books are similar in size and identical in price. Many are supported with training videos.

To order *50-MINUTE* Books and Videos or request a free catalog, contact your local distributor or Crisp Publications, Inc., 1200 Hamilton Court, Menlo Park, CA 94025. Our toll-free number is (800) 442-7477.

50-Minute Series Books and Videos Subject Areas . . .

Management
Training
Human Resources
Customer Service and Sales Training
Communications
Small Business and Financial Planning
Creativity
Personal Development
Wellness
Adult Literacy and Learning
Career, Retirement and Life Planning

Other titles available from Crisp Publications in these categories

Crisp Computer Series
The Crisp Small Business & Entrepreneurship Series
Quick Read Series
Management
Personal Development
Retirement Planning